SISTER'S WITH PURPOSE

I AM MY SISTER'S KEEPER

ERIKA T MOORE

DEDICATION

I will like to first thank God for given me the gifts and talents of writing. I am delighted to use them for your glory. I will like to dedicate this book to every woman who has ever endured hardship, disappointment, heartache and above all life and overcame every obstacle that was placed in their life. You are truly a great illustration of Phillipians 4:13, "I can do all things through Christ, which strengthens me". I pray this book can and will be used as a tool to help you advance and enhance in your spiritual walk with Christ. To my beautiful church family Praise God International Ministries, I truly love you all. This book is designed to raise awareness in the Female gender all over the world. Let's begin to encourage each other and help build each other up. I am my sister's keeper.

ACKNOWLEDGEMENTS

Many of my great blessings have come from many great Men and Women of God. I first began by thanking my beautiful mother Sandra Williams and my beautiful sister Monique Ward. I love you both with all my heart. I will like to thank the six beautiful women who found it not robbery to partake in this collaboration and share personal details with us about your life. To the two beautiful women in my life and a part of Praise God International ministries, Missionary Julia Mc Allister and her beautiful daughter, my sister Minister Elect Wanda McAllister. Words cannot express how I feel about you both. You came into my life during my transformation, and it was right on time. From day one you showed yourself to be friendly and I truly appreciate all you have done for me and my family. You ladies rock, and I am glad to have you a part of my family.

To my childhood friend, my sister Kelly Midgette. I am so glad you are here with me in my new place of life. You have encouraged me not to give up and to continue to press towards the mark of excellence. You are truly a great example of "A Virtuous Woman". Thank you for sharing your story with us. To my beautiful sister in Christ, Prophetess Rochelle Richardson. You are an amazing woman and a great friend. Your story has touched my heart in many ways and all I can say is; "But God". I admire your strength and determination to not give up. I love you sis. To my beautiful sister in Christ, Elder Alma Collins. We have truly been to the moon and back and we are still here. Still standing for Christ. I love you girl and you already know how much I admire and respect you and all you do. To my beautiful sister, who I've known since elementary school, who has taken me and my family into your family, Kathleen James-Lawrence. I thank you for taking the time out to be a part of this great movement. Through the God in you and your family, it has taught me to be steadfast.

I love and respect you and our beautiful sisters, Evette, Peggy, and Chubby (she's going to get me for this) Joy, Kean, Plychette, Tracey Gilliam and Stacey I love you ladies. You have been there for me since day one. May God continue to bless you all and your families. To my daughters; I love you all and thank god for you being my shining stars. And to the love of my life my husband Apostle Adolph Moore. I am so glad God allowed you to find me. You are truly the wind beneath my wings. You give me so much joy and I am very grateful to be your wife. I thank you all for being a part of this great book and I pray that all who reads it find peace, joy, forgiveness, deliverance and above all that they find God.

FORWARD

Do you ever get overwhelmed by challenges in life that feel too big to overcome? The problems you face will either defeat you or develop you. Has God ever tested your faith with a problem? Unfortunately, most people fail to see how God wants to use problems for good in their lives. We all have obstacles that prevent us from growing spiritually. In our own strength, we are limited; we get discouraged and deny our potential. But God has better plans. "You intended to harm me, but God intended it all for good". (Gen. 50:20, NIV). God uses problems to **DIRECT** you, sometimes God has to light a fire under you to get you moving. God uses problems to **INSPECT** you. People are like teabags, if you want to know what's inside them, drop them in hot water. God uses problems to **CORRECT** you. Some lessons we learn only through pain and failure. God uses problems to **PROTECT** you. A problem can actually be a blessing in disguise. God uses problems to **PERFECT** you. God is far more interested in your character than your comfort. There is a purpose behind every obstacle you must face. "Sister's with Purpose" share inspirational and heartfelt stories of the lives of many women and how they've overcome with God.

My hope is that you become inspired, and allow God to give you a vision of what life can look like beyond your problems.

–Kathleen James-

Lawrence

TABLE OF CONTENTS

Missionary Julia McAllister

Bio

Mother Julia has been a member of Praise God International Ministries since 2015. She has devoted and committed her life to Christ since 2007. While experiencing a lot of barriers in her life, it has built her confidence and holiness with Confirmation of faith, dedication and loyalty has extended her relationship with Jesus Christ. It has given her the ability to minister and educate her family as her spiritual walk increased her wisdom and knowledge enlarged. She is in Ministers and Leadership training and she is also the Church Mother, Elder, and Head of the Hospitality, Finance Officer, and the Apostle's Adjutant

See The Naomi In Me

By: Missionary Julia McAllister

After Naomi husband and sons died, it was like it left her the man of the family. Her daughter – in-laws followed her. Because she was committed to God. She showed respect, loyalty and love to God. I can put my family in play with Naomi and Ruth. By serving God and staying committed to him, by giving my family the respect, loyalty and love of God. That's how my mother taught me to be and to treat others. By committing to God it can help you deal with things going on in your life. My family trusts me, like Naomi daughter in- law Ruth trusted her. This is why Ruth continued to follow her even after Orphah left. By me staying committed to God, shows my grandchildren how to love God and all that is around us. All can see and feel the love that we all have for God. Loving God you have to put him first in what you do, say and live.

I teach my children that God will answer prayer as long as you believe in him and trust in him. He answers your prayers on his time and not our time. But you must remain faithful in his word. People have tendencies to follow good if good is in their hearts. When you teach your family how to love, respect and be loyal to God, so when they grow up, and go about their lives, they will remember what they've been taught at home. Just remember a family love comes from loyalty, respect. This is how Naomi daughter in law Ruth felt towards her. A family that prays together, stays together. It wasn't always easy for the two of them, especially being women in a male dominant world. They had to find food, shelter and work just to make ends meet.

This reminds me of myself when I first became a single mother of four small children. Even though my husband didn't die, I was still faced with obstacles that no mother should have to go through. It didn't always come easy for them. This is where Naomi wisdom came into play to help them to rely and depend on God as well as each other. Even though Ruth followed Naomi back to her home town, it was Ruth faith in Naomi God that allowed her to believe it for herself. She never once doubted Naomi nor did she ever complain. Even though my ex-husband deliberately refused to help us with finances, I never stopped trusting and believing in God. I can recall a time when he had the electricity shut off being that they were in his name. But what about his children? Will they not be in the dark too? Instead of complaining. I prayed to my heavenly father for guidance. He turned my attention back to all my mother has taught me when I was growing up. I thank God for wisdom.

Wisdom had me get candles that was used as a light source for me and my children to see. Wisdom had me purchase a kerosene heater that provided heat for us .As a newly single mother, I understood if I was ever going to make it out of my wilderness experience. I had to put all my trust in God. Sometimes the road we are traveling on gets very hard. Think like Naomi, trust our God. He will lighten the burdens. Our expression is, "God won't put no more on you, than you can bear". I am truly a living witness of this. Even though it may have appeared to be rain in my life more than sunshine, when I first became a single mother. God has always reigned in my life. There were times, I didn't know where our next meal was coming from. God said in his word that he will never leave me nor will he forsake me. I held on to these words, and I promise you that we never went hungry. I made sure that no

matter what I did, that I always acknowledged God and gave him
the praise, honor and glory he was entitled too. I often hear women
say; "you don't know what I'm going through or what I went
through'. The keyword is went through. You made it.

You are still standing. Who told you that everything will always be
peaches and cream? Who lied to you and said you will never go
through anything? Through my faithfulness and perseverance and
trusting God, I went on to own two beautiful homes. Hard to
believe, if you were to focus on not having lights, not having
enough money to pay bills, let alone purchase food. But I am here
to tell you in this book that I am a survivor. I am an overcomer. I
can do all things through Christ, which strengthens me, Philippians
4:13. I never allowed defeat to play a part in my life. I refused to
be a victim. I had daughters, I was raising and they were watching
me. I understood the importance of never giving up, or allowing
things to consume me that wasn't spiritual. I knew if I given up,
my daughters will follow in my footsteps. And in my heart and
mind this would not be acceptable or pleasing to me or God. The
more tired I was, the harder I pushed to go on. When people said I
wouldn't or couldn't be able to do or accomplish something. The
more determined I was to accomplish it.

I get very emotional thinking about all I've gone through. I had to
make my children believers. And the only way I knew how to do
this was to show them. I done this by trusting God and treating
people the way I desired to be treated. I am an honest woman, and
my word was my bond. It was all I had to help me survive. I thank
God that I had the foundation provided from my Mother. It
showed me the importance of having and raising my family. My
mother instilled God within me and my siblings. We may not have
had a lot of material things. But we had God and that was enough.
Yes, life threw me many curve balls. Yes I've fallen so many
times that I stopped counting. But yes, I dealt with each obstacle

with God's help and yes I made it. Today I get to enjoy the fruits of my labor. I enjoy watching my adult children live their lives. I enjoy watching my grandchildren being raised the way I taught my children. Most of all I am enjoying my life in God. So to every woman young and old who is reading this book.

Encourage the woman that are in your lives today, tomorrow and the ones who will come after you. Let them know that they matter and they are not alone. Tell your story, because what they see is the glory, but not your untold story.

Sister Cherida McAllister

Bio

Before I became a member of Praise God International Ministries in 2015, I was drawn to the diversity and welcoming environment of the church. I'm currently a Store Manager at a retail store. I bring forth my managerial skills to help guide,minister, lead, and develop members and people of the world. I'm raising two children Rasheem and Kenyia; and one adult child Le Shea. My goals are to encourage economic empowerment within the communities, enhance my faith with God and connection with my church family. Being a part of Praise God International Ministries has been one of the most awarding accomplishment in my life. By attending Praise God International Ministries, I have been blessed to get the fulfillment of my personal spiritual needs and understanding of Jesus teachings. As I begin my transformation spiritually, economically, and professionally I will always position God first in my life.

Psalm 71;7-8

My life is an example to many, because you have been my strength and protection.

That is why I can never stop praising you; I declare your glory all day long.

Why Me?

By: Sister Cherida McAllister

It all started about 21 years ago. I thought I was an independent teenager. Working a full time job, hanging in the clubs, drinking, smoking and doing everything that made me appear that I was grown. I was a healthy 125 to 130lbs teenager. I noticed that I started to lose weight and my skin had begun to darken. I was so afraid to tell my mom what I was experiencing. I decided to take upon myself and go to the doctor. I went on numerous occasions and was unsuccessful with a diagnosis. At this time my weight and skin is very noticeable to everyone. My family began to ask questions. During this time Aids had surfaced and was on television and in the news frequently. I automatically thought that I was a victim of Aids. I immediately went to my mom and asked for help. We begin our journey again to seek out a medical diagnosis.

Finally, we got an answer. I was told that I had Cancer and needed surgery. I immediately thought I was going to die. I looked up at the ceiling and said to GOD Why Me? I really didn't understand why he chose me to carry this deadly disease. I believed that there is a God but I didn't have belief in anything. My surgery was scheduled for four months out. But I had to be examined every two weeks to monitor the process. So I thought at that point there was hope. So on my two week appointment I was told that the Cancer has grown at a rapid rate and surgery was needed right away. I'm in tears once again confused and scared. I asked God once again

Why Me? I didn't think I was a bad child and I felt like I didn't deserve what I was dealing with. The surgery lasted about two hours. We hoped that it all had been removed. Only time will tell.

As I recovered from my surgery there was times when I felt like just ending my life and giving up. I didn't really pray and didn't have a relationship with God. So the Devil was messing with my mind.

As it speaks in Ephesians 4:18 – "they are darkened in their understanding and separated from the life of God because of the ignorance that is in them due to the hardening of their hearts."

During my follow up appointment I had been experiencing things with my body that I didn't understand. So we begin to research the what and why's. The Doctor comes in and tell me that I was four months pregnant. I was pregnant when I had my surgery and the Doctor didn't detect it. Okay so now I have to deal with possibly having a mentally retarded child due to the medication I had been taking and stopping my treatment because we can't continue due to the fact that I am pregnant. Getting rid of the pregnancy was not an option for me because the hospital refused to do it. My life was over as I seen it. All I could say was Why Me? I should've been enjoying life and living it up. Instead I was in tears, scared, and felt like God did not hear my cries. To make a long story short I went through my pregnancy and had a healthy child no life threatening medical conditions and God had removed the deadly disease that I was carrying. When I gave birth to my first born I then begin to realize how powerful God is and his capabilities. I begin to talk to God and not question him. I now know that God was preparing me for the next chapter in my life. Psalms 34; 17 The righteous cry out, and the LORD hears them;

He delivers them from all their troubles. I begin to attend church, read my bible and believe in God. As I continue my life journey I will never think that God has forsaken me. Even as I stand here today I have been diagnosed with a deadly Lung disease but when I go to my checkups it looks to the Doctors that the disease doesn't even exist. Just like it says in   Exodus 23:25

You shall serve the Lord your God, and he will bless your bread and your water, and I will take sickness away from among you.

I'm glad and proud to be me. I thank God for choosing me.

Thanks

Sister Cherida McAllister

Kelly Smith Midgette

Bio

Kelly Midgette is married to the love of her life Tony Midgette. Together they have four lovely children Brittany, Tone', Daija and Asa. They also adore their three grandchildren Kennedy, Zachary and Maximus. Kelly and her family are members of Raleigh International Church in Raleigh, NC. Kelly's passions are feeding the homeless and mentoring single mothers.

Kelly and Tony are the business owners of Around the Clock Cleaning, LLC. In Raleigh, NC.

My Life

By: Sister Kelly Midgette Smith

I'll show up and take care of you as I promised and bring you back home. I know what I'm doing. I have it all planned out-plans to take care of you, not abandon you, plans to give you a future you hope for. Jeremiah 29:11 The Message

July 09, 2009 was the worst day ever for me. I was sentenced to 40 months federal prison time. I was devastated and couldn't believe that I was going to prison. I couldn't fathom being without my husband and children for that long. It was the worst ever. Even though I had been committing crimes for a while it still didn't seem right that this was happening to me. This isn't supposed to happen to me because I am a good person, my parents are pastors, I take care of my children and others. I had every excuse why I shouldn't go to prison even though I know I had done wrong.

The hardest part for me was taking off my mask. I had been exposed. Everyone could see me for who I was and what I had done. I was embarrassed and humiliated at the same time. I didn't know at the time that it would get much worse. I was in for a wide awakening. For so many years I lied and kept secrets from my husband. When I had to tell him it was so hard for me. He knew something was wrong but he actually thought that I was having an affair. At this point I really wish I could just die. I would have rather died than to be exposed for what I had done.

My case had sat on the Federal prosecutor's desk for years. I had talked to her several times and my case was not even supposed to be prosecuted.

I had gotten a call from her telling me that her supervisor had been on her desk and wanted to know what she was going to do with this case. She told him her plans and he wanted it to go to the grand jury. The next call I got was the grand jury had indicted me. I went through the whole process alone and scared because I just couldn't bring myself to tell my family and friends. My husband found out when I had to wear an ankle bracelet for home confinement. I didn't know that I could hurt him the way that I did.

A couple of days before my sentencing I had a dream that my husband was driving alone in the car crying. I knew that I would not come home after sentencing because that is what God had prepared me for in the dream. On the day of sentencing the attorney kept telling me" no matter what happens in court today you will go home and they will send you a date to turn yourself in." I wanted to believe him but I knew I wouldn't because I was already shown what was going to happen. When the judge sentenced me to 40 months I just collapsed. I couldn't believe that she would give me that much time and again I just wanted to die. Death seemed so much better than where I was going to end up.

I never knew what it was like to be chained like a dog or some wild animal. They shackled me like I was going someplace. I didn't have the privilege of just going to prison; they wanted me to take the scenic route. I went to four different jails. I have ridden on Conair. Nothing I had done seemed worth any of this. The jails were disgusting and dirty. Some of them had one toilet in the middle of the floor. Of course at some point you would have to go. That was a humiliating experience in itself.

I was told that once I made it to prison it would be better. I didn't know if I should believe that or not. None of it seemed great to me. This was something that I just couldn't accept even though it was happening whether or not I accepted it.

Going through the jails I did meet some really nice women that I had a lot in common with. One thing I found out was most of the women locked up were molested. They had been molested by their mother's boyfriends, uncles, friends of the family, brothers and cousins. I listened to their stories and cried with them. It seemed like everyone had a story to tell. It broke my heart to hear some of them. They had turned to drugs and alcohol to ease their pain. At that point I wondered why I had done the things that I had done. After all I am smart; why would I do something so wrong?

On August 28, 2009 I finally arrived in Alderson, WV. Some want to call it Camp Cupcake but that isn't what I wanted to call it. I arrived at the airport and was picked up by a van and driven to the prison. I arrived in R&D, I was screened, assigned a bed and given a bag with some personal stuff and changed into a jumpsuit. I was told to go up the hill to the housing units. I thought we would be taken there but the free rides were over. All I would do for the rest of my time was walk. I went and found my building and my bed assignment. I was in a room called the fishbowl. It was nicknamed that because it was glass and everyone who walked by could look in and they did. It was there that I met some friends that would be my friends even now. We have a bond that no one else understands.

I remember my first time going to breakfast alone and looking out at the mountains crying Lord why? That is when He told me why. He sent me there to save my life. He wanted to know if I trusted Him but I didn't, I couldn't. I couldn't trust anyone.

13

I did not do my time gracefully. I had a hard time adjusting. The friends that went through orientation with me at one point abandoned me. They had all come to terms that this was happening and they accepted what was going on. It took me almost until I left to get with the program. It was that time alone that I got close with God; my time did go a lot smoother.

For the first time in my life I was alone. I had two sisters growing up. My mom had my third sister when I was 16yrs. old. I was with my sisters when I was not in school. My mom was a single mother and worked a lot to make ends meet. So I had to be responsible for them and make sure that everything was straight when my mother came home from work. I became a mother myself when I was 19 years old. I found that I never wanted to be alone. I had been taking care of people all my life it seemed. It took going to prison before I had time for myself. I got to just focus on me for once. Nothing else mattered because I couldn't control anything at that time. I needed a break from my life and I didn't even know it!

I started going to the chapel for religious services. There were some awesome women and men of God that would come in and minister to us. They would spend their own money to come and worship with us. I thought that was amazing that anyone would do that. The services were awesome and really helped me keep it together because after all this was the hardest thing I ever had to do. I really got into the word of God, studying and praying. God really revealed himself to me at this time. I started having more dreams than ever. There was nothing that happened at home that my God didn't prepare me for before calling home. That was awesome! I was a friend of God. He helped me with issues that I had and some of them I didn't even realize that I had. He really knew what He was doing sending me to prison. It still wasn't easy but I could at least cope.

The women that I met in the chapel were on fire for the Lord. They could pray and prophesy. The prison had different choirs and those girls could sing. I used my time by immersing myself in the word. I was at every service. I spent so much time in the chapel; if there was no services going on I would read and listen to music. The chapel was my favorite place to be. The worship was pure and true. That is when I learned that I could trust Him!

Once I started trusting everything just changed. My attitude was better and I learned a new hobby. I learned to crotchet and I was very good at it. I was making and selling bags, blankets, and pillows. I got into a daily routine that started with Morning Prayer. I was in prayer three times a day on my knees. I would make time for exercise twice a day. I would crotchet in between those times. These things were very therapeutic for me. I would sit and be at peace with myself. I would use that time to examine my life and where I was headed. I knew that I needed to know my expected end before I left Alderson.

My family's life had also been impacted because of my incarceration. When a loved one goes to prison they are physically away but the whole family does time. This was the part that bothered me the most. My family had to suffer because of me. I needed to be away but I really missed them. I only got to see them three times and I did twenty eight month in Alderson, WV. I think that it is what they needed as well. My husband started to attend church services every Sunday. He would go to early morning prayer. My pastor prophesied to him telling him that" this had to happen; God needed me out the way to get to him!" That blew my mind and my husband really received that message. It really seemed like we were all winning at this point. We were all falling into the place where God wanted us to be for the first time.

During my incarceration the Lord would give me so many dreams that dealt with all the issues that I had in the past. Those dreams helped in an indescribable way; growing up I never felt good enough or pretty enough. It seems like my whole life I was in some competition. One dream that I had was that I was looking at houses with my husband. In the dream I couldn't understand why I was looking at this house because I already had a house.

The house was very similar to the house that we were buying at the time. The very next day while doing my exercise I received an email from my daughter that dad needed me to call home. I called home and my husband gave me the news that he couldn't hang on to the house. I comforted him in telling him that it was okay because I saw another house in my dream last night that was very similar to our house. At this point we had lost everything from our home, business and vehicle. I had a sister in prison that didn't know me prophesy that I needed to let my house go because that was not Gods best for me. That house was the nicest house ever!

Another great dream that I had was I was in an orchard field. My family and I were passing out pretty red apples. Apples were everywhere; on the ground in baskets and still on the tree. Anyone that came to us would get a basket of these beautiful apples. I sent my dreams to a lady in my church; she has the gift of interpretation. She said that my dream meant that "my family and I will give from our abundance, not from what we need to survive but from our overflow." I know for me I have always been a giver but I have also had to be a borrower.

Through this journey I have learned so many things. One thing for sure I wish that I would have embraced what was going on and trusted God from the beginning. I did gain so many gifts and have been delivered from so many of my issues in the twenty eight months that I served.

Patience was a big one for me since I was in control of everything or at least I thought I was. Being in control has always been big for me. It's almost like I never trusted anyone to lead me. This wasn't good for my marriage either. I felt like no one could do it like me!

My testimony is this. God sent me into the wilderness and with a forty month sentence. I couldn't trust Him in the beginning but eventually I couldn't do it by myself. I had no other choice. I tried it my way and it wasn't working for me. I was released on January 5, 2012.

Since I have been home my God has restored everything that was lost. We have a beautiful new home two doors down from the house we lost. Our business is thriving and I have a brand new car. We are happier than ever before because of this experience. We had to go through some things and it was not easy but it was worth it. We didn't know what the reward would be or even if it would be a reward. We know that our God is faithful and He loves us. I am so grateful for a family that loved me and supported my husband and children through this tribulation period.

Alma Collins Thomas

Bio

Alma Collins Thomas is an ordained Minister Educator, Motivational speaker, playwright, author. She holds two B.S degrees one in Human Services with a concentration and children and families and a BS in Christian Studies. She is a contributor writer for Authentically You and Lasum online magazines. She is the co-author of BAD heels and Love Marriage and Divorce. She is currently working on her two debut books Dream Killers and From the waiting room to the recovery room. She is the single mother of two children Sabria and Tysean who left his earthly home to reign in his heavenly home in 2009.

Dream Killer

By: Minister Alma Collins

The thief cometh not, but for to steal, and to kill, and to destroy: I am come that they might have life, and that they might have it more abundantly.

In John 10:10 we see that the thief's desire is to come, to steal, kill and destroy The enemy recognizes that God has a plan for your life. One of my favorite people in the Bible is Joseph. Joseph was a dreamer and he had a lot of haters in his life. Joseph had a dream concerning his brothers and they got upset when he told them about the dream and they plotted to kill him. They wanted to animate the anointing that Joseph had on his life. It was more than that multicolored coat that he received from his father, but it was what that coat represented that they wanted to destroy the father's anointing on his life. Do you realize that people will hate on you because of the anointing that you have on your life?

All of my life I had to face hater after hater and I just could not understand why people hated on me, in the natural sense I didn't have anything but a dollar and a dream. I was barely existing living from paycheck to paycheck surviving on just enough and people that seemingly had it going on was always hating on me. I started my own personal journey from dreamer to visionary, God began to reveal to me what was happening in my life and it wasn't me per se but the anointing that was on my life. They saw the anointing on my life before I did but what they did not see was all the hell that I have gone through for this anointing. The fire that was meant to burn up my destiny. When Joseph dreamed that one day his brother would bow down to him, the enemy stepped in and tried to eradicate the dream and the dreamer. It's important to understand that the adversary will only try to massacre your dreams when you are in the process of making your day dreams into a vision, the enemy only gets stir up when he realizes that you are more than just a dreamer.

He doesn't care how much time you waste in lull land, the enemy and his kingdom are not threatened by your just dreaming about sharing your life changing testimony with the world, it is when you stop being a wannabe that is you better watch out because now the enemy is after you. The enemy was sitting on the sidelines just laughing his behind off when I was just talking about all of the ideas that God was placing in my spirit. The enemy and my dream killers would constantly ask me with a smirk on their faces how is that book coming along. But when I started to write this book and I fell some many chains falling off of me, it was then that the devil got mad as hell at me. So you need to understand that you are no threat to the enemy while you are just talking about writing a book, finishing school or starting a business the devil is just laughing at you.

But I dare you to enroll in school, get and EIN number or start writing that book, just do something to make your dream into a reality, you need to start to make plans to bring that dream to manifestation. The devil doesn't mind you sleeping but it is when you wake up that you become armed and dangerous. It's when you wake up that you aggravate the devil and that is when you become a marked target for assassination. The devil and his imps have barraged you with assaults and you have wondered, will it ever get any better! Will things ever change for me and my household? I have been talked about, I have been physically and mentally sick. I have been ostracized and banished from some who I used to call friend all because they hated on my anointing. I was told from a little girl that I wasn't going to make it and that I would never amount to anything. Been down and heard it so long until you wonder, "Will I always be on the bottom, will I always be behind, and will I ever do any better than I am right now!"

The Apostle Paul says in Romans 8:37 "No, in all things we are MORE than conquerors through Him who loved us." We're not JUST conquerors, but he says that we are more than conquerors through Jesus Christ! There is absolutely nothing that the devil can send our way that can defeat us! People will and have put you in a box. They have labeled you. Let's see some of the labels: Poor, broken home, AA, old, fat, no child, no degree, divorced, single, depressed, kids on drugs, husband alcoholic, and poor family background. I t's time for you to get out of the box You have to learn how to fight all these stereotypes that you have been labeled in your life. As you are reading this book I need you to high five yourself and declare I am getting out of this box. Yes, "I'm getting out of this box, because I am destined for greatness! Many of you today do not realize just how close you are to the success or greatness God has destined for you.

There is a dream in you that is bigger than you that is really the real you – that's the destined for greatness God has deposited. You may be down at the moment but honey this too shall pass. This will be a part of your past. This will be part of your testimony. Down is not your destiny. Some of you've had trouble coming at you from every angle. The Lord has promised in His Word to make us the victor and not the victim. Beloved I believe the entire Word of God and I know that the rain falls on the just and on the unjust, but I also believe the promises of God that tell us that we are going to overcome and we will not be defeated Deuteronomy 28 states "All these blessings will come upon you and accompany you if you obey the Lord your God.. You will be blessed in the city and in the country.

The fruit of your womb will be blessed, and the crops of your land and the young of your livestock. You will be blessed when you come in and blessed when you go out. The Lord will grant that the enemies who rise up against you will be defeated before you.

They will come at you from one direction but flee from you in seven. (He'll Break them UP!) The Lord will send His blessing upon your barns and everything you put your hand to God will bless you in the land that He's giving to you. The Lord will establish you as His holy people as He's promised you on oath, if you keep the commands of the Lord your God and walk in His ways. The Lord will open up the heavens, the storehouse of His bounty, to send rain on your land in season and to bless all the work of your hands. You will lend too many nations, but will borrow from none. The Lord, will make YOU the head, and not the tail. If you pay attention to the commands of the Lord your God, that I give you this day and carefully follow them, you will always be at the top and never at the bottom. "I'm telling you today, that you may be low and it may seem like you're on the very bottom, but let me tell you that you aren't on the bottom Others quit but you held on. Others ran away, but you stood your ground. While others walked away you remained. While others lost faith, your faith remained strong.

Now God says it's your "due season!" One of the hardest trials that I had to endure was the loss of my only son. Everyone that was close to me thought I was going to lose my mind or kill myself and their prophecies almost came to pass. I remember the day that I was going to take my life. I was standing in the kitchen with a bottle of pills in my hand about to take them all and I heard a still voice whisper if you do it you will never see him again because he is in paradise. I put the pills back on the shelf and started on a slow road to recovery. The word due means: it is owed to you. Because of your faithfulness God says, "I owe you something! I owe you a blessing! I owe you a promotion! I owe you a reward!" The reward you are getting ready to receive will be greater than any trial, affliction, or setback that you have experienced. God is going to give you double for your trouble and your future is going to be greater than your past!

I am so excited for the women that are reading this book right now because your life is about to change You not just coming out of what you've been in, you're coming out blessed greater than you've ever been blessed. You're getting ready to have things you didn't even have when you went in. You stayed faithful and now the page is turning. Your situation is changing. Your miracle has begun. A new chapter is beginning. Regardless of what you may see or how you may feel your greater days are ahead. It doesn't matter what has happened in your life or what is happening at the present time- you're greater is coming because you are a sister with purpose. God has a plan and a purpose for your life and no matter what has happened in your past God still has a plan for your life.

Rochelle Richardson

Bio

Ma'ri J, (Rochelle Richardson), is a Entrepreneur, Health and Wellness Coach, and Founder of Transcendent Life Managements, an organization designed to work with communities to help people surpass the ordinary expectations of life by transforming minds, bodies, and souls through health and wellness awareness. She helps people see the importance of health due to obesity and unhealthy eating, maintaining a healthy mental state, and developing a relationship with Jesus Christ.

Ma'ri J has always enjoyed starting and running businesses. In fact, by the time she was 14, she had already began her journey of entrepreneurship by mowing yards, washing cars, and helping elderly people in her small community.

I am the owner of Transcendent Health which provides health and wellness, weight loss, beauty, performance enhancement, gourmet coffee, energy and longevity, and shape wear in partnership with Total Life Changes. To name a few of the products which enabled my business to grow daily is the Iaso Detox Tea, Nurtaburst, and NRG. Iaso Detox Tea enables customers to detox their system by filtrating toxins and chemical caused by the food we eat and the air we breathe. Nurtraburst is a liquid multivitamin supplement and a high source of digestive enzymes which is absorbs into the bloodstream. NRG is a energy supplement with a blend of synergistic ingredient and key support minerals. NRG is an all-natural supplement that can sustain itself for hours.

I got into this line of business in 2015 when I was trying to find myself following a divorce from a marriage of almost 20 years. My favorite part of having a home-based business is freedom. It allows me to set my own hours, still be available for my family and friends, and helping people find the way back to healthy living.

When I am not working on Transcendent Health, I like to spend time with my family and friends, movies, eating out, and reading. I am devoted daughter, mother, and writer from Bethlehem, Texas.

I think of myself as being humbled, outgoing, ambitious person, although I've also been known to speak the truth in love when I am asked to speak on a particular subject.

The things I love in life the most is enjoying time with my three children, La'Darius, 22, Kirren, 19, and Shae, 17 and my granddaughter Majestee, spending time in fellowship with my brothers and sisters at Destiny World outreach Center, and growing daily as a business owner.

What's Your Problem?

By: Rochelle Richardson

Great afternoon. I was asked to collaborate along with other women in a book sharing our experiences dealing with our deliverance and the experience. This is just my chapter. It's long and I hope I don't lose you in the reading. I had to copy and paste it into an email because I did on Mac notes.

What's Your Problem?

I am so grateful God has brought me back to the place where He originally ordained and purposed for me to be. The past three years I have been through nothing short of hell. After such a great fall, how can anyone find their way back to God?

I had lost myself in addictions such as sex, alcohol, and drugs. I had to make a decision to finally let all those things which had hindered me go. It wasn't easy, but the Holy Spirit continued to speak to me through different people even in the midst of my sin. See, I didn't leave God, I left the church. I was embarrassed because my husband at the time and I were ordained deacons. I was ministering through miming, serving in different capacities in ministry, but I took a detour to mask the pain I was going through. Then one day right before the New Year of 2016, He spoke so loud and clear it scared me. No, honestly I hadn't heard the Holy Spirit speak, well let me say it like this. He was speaking loud and clear, but I wasn't listening. He asked me one question, and from that day my life started to transform. The question was so simple, "What's your problem?"

I can remember hearing this question, and was awaken from sleep. I tend to lay in the bed as my daughter is preparing

for school. I jumped out the bed thinking my daughter was asking me this question. I was in shock my body was trembling like I had been on the scariest roller coaster of my life. For years, I have been chasing after something I thought I needed. Wow, how did I get to this place of feeling desperate? What me, desperate? How had I allowed my soulish desires to overtake the understanding of my purpose and destiny? Why had I chosen to step away from a Man who loves me without any conditions?

I have asked myself these questions for years, only to find out the problem was within me. What do I mean by within me? It was a spirt of lust. Oh, this spirit is notorious, overwhelming, controlling, and will stop at nothing when it come to devaluing God's worth. For the past year and a half, lust kept me away from being in my place of purpose. The problem was simple, I had renewed my relationship with Christ over and over again, but I hadn't renewed my mind.

I desired to feel love from a man, and really only God could give me the love I needed. My mind was still stuck in a "cheating place" I had created over 12 years ago. What is a cheating place? Mentally I hadn't been faithful to my husband during the course of our marriage, so what made me think I was going to be faithful to God; in anyway. Even though I was doing my best to stay in the will of God, the mental cheating place combined with my imaginations made it easier naturally for me to jump in and out of bed with different men, constantly. I had become a lust-driven woman due to the mental adultery committed for so many years.

Mental adultery and a heart full of lust, pain, anger, and forgiveness was a lethal combination.

What is mental adultery? I am so glad you asked. Mental adultery is having intercourse with your husband naturally, and having intercourse with someone else mentally.

Wow, let's take a few seconds and read this line one more time. I was having intercourse naturally with my husband, but mentally having intercourse with someone else.

Proverbs 23:7 states, "for as he thinks in his heart, so is he. As one who reckons, he says to you eat and drink, yet his heart is not with your [but is grudging the cost]". (Amplified version) Ma'ri, what are you saying? I am saying exactly what the scripture is saying. I was mentally cheating on my husband. Wait, I was a believer, a woman of wisdom, truth, and knowledge, filled with the Holy Spirit. How did this mentally adultery become so precedent in my life. The word mental in definition means: of or relating to the mind, carried out by or taking place in the mind. We will use the latter part of the definition for clarity alone with Proverbs 23:7. I was sinning in my imaginations.

What a man thinks in his heart, so is he; that was the first problem. I was lusting for other men. I didn't think it was so until I started having more and more dreams about the men. I mean, I would wake up in a full sweat with the evidence of sexual activity. I don't think I need to say anything else. I had opened a door for Incubus, and being new in Christ I didn't understand anything about Incubus. I would wake up with scratches on my body, hands touching me, and even felt penetration. Using my imagination to create and carry out these adventures in my mind was not only a bad choice, but a sin. Did I ever think about the consequences of these imaginations? Not at all, I was working so hard not to carry them out naturally, but I was already in my cheating place with a demon.

Can you image having intercourse with a person and mental intercourse with another at the same time. I was exhausted, and can recall one night in the middle of being intimate with my husband I actually called the other man's name. Oh, my goodness. Was the intercourse in my imagination so vivid and clear that I was in total action with this other man? This is exactly what I mean by the spirit of lust being notorious.

This man was real in my imagination. I could feel him touching and kissing me, whispering in my ear, and yes making me feel like I had never felt before. Well, actually it wasn't a man it was a spirit having his way with me in the course of an intimate moment with the man I had vowed not to cheat on. My husband realized what I had said, and body without any thoughts of how he would feel I told him I was thinking about another man. I am so grateful God covered me with His protection because my husband could have snapped, and Ma'ri could have been history.

Mark 7:21-23, states "for from within, [that is] out of the hearts of men, come base and wicked thoughts, sexual immortality, stealing, murder, adultery, coveting, (a greedy desire to have more wealth), dangerous and destructive wickedness, deceit; unrestrained (indecent) conduct; an evil eye (envy), slander (evil speaking, malicious, misrepresentation, abusiveness, pride, (the sin of uplifted hearts against God and man), foolishness (follow, lack of sense, recklessness, thoughtlessness). All these evil [purposes and desires] come from within, and they make the man unclean and render him unhallowed". These scriptures are the very reason why soul ties must be broken. See, the man in my imagination was real in the natural. He was a young man I had an affair with, and even though physically I couldn't have him I made sure mentally I did.

Wow, mental sin. Do I really need to say anything else after the bible has given us such clarity? The

Spirit of lust within me was being fed by my thoughts. I was quietly murdering myself, and being deceitful to my husband and God. How was I being deceitful to God? In this season of my life, as I mentioned before, I was a baby in Christ with enough knowledge of God's word to know better than allowing my thoughts to carry out such mental actions. We must know the worse battle we fight is in our minds.

Just a little background on how the spirit of lust entered into my marriage. Thinking back to the beginning of our relationship it was founded on lust. From the first time I seen my husband, I wanted him. Every time I laid eyes on him I thought about having sex with this man. Our eyes locked in 1992 as he was leaving for Europe, and I was entering Basic Training. I would tell my battle buddies, "That's my husband", and yes he did become my husband, but God's love was never established. Once we married we thought love was between the sheets. I guess that would explain two beautiful daughters 14 months apart. You get the picture. Let's move along.

Here I was a woman who had been married for almost twenty years, now divorced, and didn't know if I was coming or going. I was so lost, and although there was some cheating the first few years of our marriage, I had been emotionally, physically, and mentally tied to this man since I was twenty. What we didn't know or understand is we were planting seeds of discord over our marriage. We never asked forgiveness of each other, which lead to us bringing up the cheating being thrown up every time we wanted to hurt each other. We through the past like a quarterback passing the ball for a long forty yard pass. It was more like a hot potato. Your remember the game. We would pass the hurt and pain, back and forth, back and forth to one another until we were either so angry we he would leave the house, or I realized after breaking dishes they would have to be replaced.

We were young without guidance, and didn't desire to have any because hurting each other felt like sipping on some fine wine. Now, here I am after almost 19 years trying to deal with these fumbles. I didn't understand how so many words were attached to me until my soul and flesh was speaking louder than the spirit.

Yes, I should want to feel love again at least that's what my little mind was thinking. What happened was I should have never tried to know what love was in the first place. Our foundation was shaky from the beginning. The love described in I Corinthians 13 was the love I didn't know. Unconditional love as something lust wouldn't allow me to feel. Lust desired for me to live a life of emptiness, feeling as if no one could love me unless I was laying prostate, and I am not talking about being in prayer with the Lord As long as hurt was given to me hurt was given back. What I didn't realize was my G-spot had become a garden for lust to multiply and divide.

Yeah, I said it. The G-spot. Well, you are almost finished with the chapter, so if the term offends you, then the latter is for you. Oh, I am praising God already for the chains being broken from the mindset of Christian women. You want to know what G-Spot mean, yeah you ready. It is Your God spot. Oh, I can hear the chains breaking!! Yes I am speaking every word with power and authority which is in my given by God. There is no way, Ma'ri would have ever thought of God spot. I am sitting here trembling as I type these words from the Holy Spirit, Yes God use me as a willing vessel to set the captives free. What you say, I am breaking free myself. What type of ending were you looking for? The Holy Spirit knows exactly what the women of this generation need to hear. What have allowed men to play and devalue our God spot long enough?

This word was given to me in the midst of my deliverance when my eyes were closed by pain. I was lying in bed crying because I had allowed lust to put me on my back again. During this time, I was starting to desire what I missed the most, my relationship with God. How did I get here, again? I jumped in the shower crying my eyes out because I was tired of sleeping with different men, and still being left empty. As I said before, when the Holy Spirit asked me what was my problem I knew then it was time to get myself together for real.

Lust had lain dormant for so many years, as I committed mental adultery. I had given the Holy Spirit an eviction notice, and moved Him out the God spot. I had been seeking God to fill the void in my heart. At this point in my life I was desperate like a dog looking for water. The spot where God belonged was full of imaginations of what I thought love was. Our God spot is where His love resides. We have this falsified perception of what love is, and that is why it was so easy for me to commit mental adultery for almost fifteen years. Lust was my purpose killer. I had to realize what was truly happening to me. The more time I spent lusting after men I was giving my purpose killer a chance to deposit unholy things into my God spot. I devalued God's purpose within me, and the war between my flesh and the Spirit began. The spot as women where we desire to be stimulated is OUR PURPOSE. Holy Spirit You better use me. I can only talk about me and what filled my God spot.

Remember I had been married for almost 20 years, and now divorced with so much residue within me it was ridiculous. When the Holy Spirit revealed to me the entire time I was having sex with these different men, drinking, and smoking I was looking for my purpose, my God spot, I was floored. I was seeking the place where I had gotten out of line, and lost the stimulation from God. I started to pray more, read my bible more, and attending service every time the doors opened. Now, here I am sharing my journey with other women in writing. I am so grateful for Gods' grace and mercy that He held my spot.

Well, it does belong to Him. If you don't remember anything from this writing, please don't allow a purpose killer keep you from your God spot. Take an inventory, and see what has taken residence in your God spot. Remember the scriptures provided in this chapter. Seek God for purpose, fight for purpose, die for purpose. Don't allow false imaginations stimulate

'The Purposed God spot". Repent, ask God for forgiveness, go on a fast, build a sisterhood of women who you now will not hold you accountable. Your God spot is waiting on you.

Rochelle Richardson

Transcendent Health, CEO

Beyond The Veil

By: Pastor Erika T. Moore

The mask I've worn is a familiar mask worn by those who suffer with "Identity Issues". This disease is very common in our society today. In my walk in life I've come across many people, who will tell me, "You don't understand what I'm going through. Or you wouldn't understand because you're light-skinned or you are pretty and my favorite is, you never had to worry about stuff like this because you've got it going on". I use to cry when I heard things like this. Now I laugh because I am an overcomer of my "Identity Issues". The biggest fallacy in my life was the lies I allowed myself to believe before deliverance set in. I use to pretend that I knew everything, but I was dying mentally, emotionally, physically and spiritually. And trust me when I say, it was definitely a slow death. "How come no one loves me," I use to cry. How come I can't get a man that will stay with me? I use to constantly wonder.

What am I doing wrong Lord God to be so alone? Depression was calling my name. I knew if I was to ever give into it, then the grave will be next for me. The harder I fought to try to get a grip, the more the weight of the world was beating me down. Not only am I a single mother of five girls. I was trying to make a dollar out of fifteen cents, which I was fifteen cents short. Not knowing my true worth forced me to listen, lean and depend on others for advice and wisdom. This caused a major catastrophe for me in my household. How can I help my family grow when I don't even know who I am? This left me feeling trapped and alone. People who I thought was my friends, I thought I can trust betrayed me in the worse way. Looking back today it is my fault.

Have I known who I was and believed in me. I would not have been trying to buy love in people, to just tolerate me. Because I was in identity crisis, this caused me to make emotional decisions in every area of my life. I was living my life of my fantasies. I recall staring in the mirror talking to myself as if I was famous or someone of great importance. This behavior only made me feel worse because I lacked the confidence I needed to go get what I want. Every year I will make the same broken promises to myself, that this will be the year that I achieve all of my dreams. Year after year, after year, after year passed by and I am still stuck in my identity crisis. I truly thought that material things will make me happy. Not true. It only made me feel worse because the world was evolving. People around me were growing. But for me I remained in the mask, which I super glued on. I wasn't going anywhere because I enjoyed the man made prison I placed myself in. One may say today, but you're a Pastor. You mentor women all over. How can this be? Well before ministry I was Erika. A woman from Long Island New York, who didn't believe in herself.

We normally hit rock bottom before we get up and climb to the mountain top. I am reminded of the story of Joseph, how his brothers sold him into slavery. They didn't know his destiny was tied in the pit experience he endured. My destiny, my ministry was tied into my insecurities and low self-esteem. My story isn't about being strung out on drugs, alcohol, gambling. My story is about the lies I lived that consumed me. I was so tired of being with men who didn't love me. I was so tired of not be accepted by my family. I was going to show them by any means necessary that I am somebody. Now this sounds so good, don't it? Well not good enough to adhere to it, because that's what I was good at. Talking. I didn't have enough of the self-afflicted pain I was indulging in. I still continued to travel down the road of misery. I dated out of conveinence instead of love.

And above all I was on my way to hell through the church. I can honestly say it took the death of a Man that I was living with. For God to get my attention. I felt so lost and restricted. I never lost anyone that close to me, I felt like my heart was ripped out from my chest. All I can do is cry and cry. It was then I taken a vow to serve God with all my heart. It was then God changed my name and everything about me was changing too. I no longer desired to be in a relationship where God wasn't the center. My ministry was birthed in the time of my transformation. I am preaching, singing and for the first time in my life I am enjoying living my life. I had a new outlook and perspective for the rest of my life. I no longer looked for love in the wrong places. I wasn't desperate for a man I was happy with me.

I no longer desired to surround myself with a group of people just so I wouldn't be alone or to have something to do. I enjoyed the quietness and spending time at home with my family. In order for God to get the glory out of my life, I had to be in my pit experience in order for me to truly see God for who he is. I couldn't hear him with the mask I was wearing. I had to go way beyond the veil to seek him in his holiness. God it's me standing in the need of prayer. God forgive me for not trusting you. God I need you. I want to live God. I want to love the way you love. And I desire to see things through your eyes. I was hurting because I never had the confidence or the push I needed to pursue any of my dreams. So I kept them hidden. Even when I written "A Mother's Time to Heal', back in Two thousand and five. I never did anything with it. It will be eight years later, when I met my now husband, who read my manuscript and decided, it was time we launch our baby. He was the first man ever to sow into me spiritually. He planted positive seeds which he waters daily. Imagine if I stayed stuck. I would have missed out on one of the greatest opportunities in my life. For the first time in my life I know how it feels to be loved by a man.

I truly thank God for all of my blessings. I share my story because many see my glory but don't know my story. So if you ever see me praising God, or crying just know its tears of joy and gratitude. Jesus loves me so much that he's again given me another chance of life. I now view things differently from the way I once did. So for all my beautiful sisters who reads this book?

Please take heed and do a self-evaluation of your life and the direction its heading. Don't allow the pressure and weight of the world back you into a corner. Believe in yourself and learn to trust and lean on God. One of my favorite scriptures that you'll always hear me recite is Psalms 34:1" I will bless the Lord at all times and his praises shall continually be in my mouth". I recite this daily as a reminder of who God is and what he has done and will do for me. It's important that the Female gender recognize who they are and their worth. For the mother's reading this book who believes their only purpose is to breed children. There is more to your life than just having children. Please know you are fearfully and wonderfully made in the image of God. Yes you may be a mother but what about your dreams, visions you have for yourself that you pushed in the back of your spiritual closet?

Now is the time for you to do you Go back to school if you desire. It's never too late. Pursue your dreams. Write them down and check them off as you complete each item on your list. Don't allow your right now situation to determine your future. To the young women who believe their only purpose is to get a man and he will provide for you. This is not what God has intended for you my love. You are more than a trophy. God designed us beautiful inside and outside. You are intelligent, beautiful, kind. You are my sister and yes I care so much about you, that I made it my business to watch out for each and every one of you. What is the plan before marriage? Even the Proverbs Thirty-one woman had a plan for her family and their future. Most women lose themselves in their marriage and children because they didn't know how to balance their life.

Whatever you desire to do you can do it. Stop using your bodies as a weapon to subdue a man and to get what you want. You will never be satisfied. We need God back in the household. We need God in our families. It is the job of every woman to educate their families about God. Don't you know we are mothers before we become mothers? From the moment we learn of our pregnancies, we began talking, singing to our unborn child. Children are impressionable. So yes Mothers we are our children first teachers. So let's get back to teaching them about Christ. Cover our families daily in prayer and develop a sound relationship with Christ and above all trust him. Even when it doesn't seem like it's there. Know God is always there. Stop lying to yourself and began to know your true worth, your true identity. My name is Erika T. Moore and I am a child of the most high and only God. Low self-esteem has been removed from me along with the guilt of others. I now spend my time teaching and educating women all over how to love themselves first so they can freely love their husbands and children.

Made in the USA
Middletown, DE
22 December 2021

56876264R00027